Watch Us Burn

Poems for a Lost Earth

Watch Us Burn

Poems for a Lost Earth

by

Gene Twaronite

Cover design by Shay Culligan
Cover image "Danger of Forest Fires," courtesy
of Gerd Altmann, under the public domain
Earth image by Wahyu Setyanto on Unsplash

ISBN: 979-8-90146-972-9
Library of Congress Control Number: 2026940344

Kelsay Books
502 South 1040 East, A-119
American Fork, Utah 84003
Kelsaybooks.com

To all who continue to fight for the Earth
and know there is no Plan B

More Praise for *Watch Us Burn*

At this late hour for nature, the insistent beating heart of the wild finds a voice in Gene Twaronite's offerings. This stirring collection—poignant, reflective and sometimes wry and funny—is a reminder of the hidden, natural worlds that often exist in our proximity but rarely receive deep consideration. *Watch Us Burn* calls on each of us to look closer, care more, and do better by this beautiful, beleaguered place.

—Mike Stark, author of *Starlings: The Curious Odyssey of a Most Hated Bird* and *Chasing the Ghost Bear: On the Trail of America's Lost Super Beast*

Acknowledgments

Thank you to the following publications, where versions of these poems previously appeared:

The Arizona Republic (Poetry Spot): “Cause of Death Unknown”
Death at the Mall (Kelsay Books, 2024): “A Terrible Beauty,” “Dethroned,” “Distress,” “Lives of a Leaf,” “Reenactment,” “The Under Story,” “To See Further”
The Museum of Unwearable Shoes (Kelsay Books, 2018): “Canyon Stories,” “Evolution,” “Feeling the Heat,” “Ode to Lucy”
New Myths: “Future Portrait of Dark Matter,” “Imaginary Garden,” “Plea for an Imaginary Amphibian,” “Pluck’d in a Far-off Land,” “Untainted”
ONE ART: a journal of poetry: “Ode to a Fake Plant”
Parks and Points: “Teddy Bear Kingdom”
Poetry Porch: “Lizard Light”
Shopping Cart Dreams (Kelsay Books, 2022): “Arms at Ninety-Five,” “By Different Boats,” “Sanctuary,” “Thermoregulation,” “Tossing Toads”
Sisyphus: “Perceptible Increments”
Sky Island Journal: “Surprises,” “Time for Sale”
Snowy Egret: “Pterodactylus”
Tipton Poetry Journal: “Flowering Means Nothing,” “What Do Trees Talk About,” “Willed to Science”
Trash Picker on Mars (Kelsay Books, 2016): “Approaching Lye Brook,” “Holy Ghost on a Window,” “Shades from the Chasm”
What the Gargoyle Sees (Kelsay Books, 2020): “Extinction Sale”

And special thanks to Kate Robinson, of Starstone Editorial, whose eagle eye sees all.

Contents

What Do Trees Talk About?

Now that we know how they signal each other
through root hairs and fungal threads of meaning,
will we ever learn to read these signals
and know what it is they talk about
in the dark loamy layers below?

Surely there must be more
to their talk than survival
as when insects or fires threaten,
just as we sapiens came to learn
grunts and guttural sounds could signify
so much more than danger
when wolves or tigers were near
but . . .

what I want to know is
do they ever sweet talk each other
sending love notes to nearby birches
as they bend in the breeze
and sing praises to Mother Tree
who watches over all?

Do they speak in hushed tones
of what it must be like to walk
on feet or touch each other
the way those wise apes do
and wonder if trees will
ever learn to read their signals
when words are too shallow and coarse

for root hairs to hear
and smoke signals fill the valleys
with the scent of disaster?

Lizard Light

All that remained
was a wisp
of bones—

beads of vertebrae
arching the spine
behind its skull.

Baring tiny teeth,
it gapes with empty
sockets at the sun

shining through the
windows of its
ivory chapel.

Imaginary Garden

imaginary gardens with real toads in them
—Marianne Moore, *Poetry*

As you enter, you see only
disorder and confusion,
devoid of any unity or meaning, but look

closer and you discover the faint
outline of a theme previously hidden in
the undergrowth, though not one

sign giving a plant's name as if that
could tell you what life is all about
for a petunia or boojum in this

garden of beauty and grotesquerie
where orchid thoughts grow side by side with
corpse flowers and creeping devil cacti,

and the withered gray stems and stalks
of the departed still rustle
in the wind.

Here a fern can fiddle,
free to unfurl into a frond or find
a wholly different shape to life,

the sweet tart taste of an apple
or the soft leathery touch of a sequoia
can sustain you for a day,

the wake-robin's rotten flesh smell
can teach you to extend your antennae
and know the world like a fly,

and the sight of a lone white violet blooming against
a green mossy cushion in a dark wood can suddenly
make you feel as if walking on sacred ground.

If you sit quietly beside a small breeding pool
as birches, maples, and willows leaf out in spring,
you might just glimpse a line of tiny

imaginary toads emerging,
waiting for someone to enter and conceive them
so they can become real.

The Under Story

When I look at trees,
I see no faces,
no trace of anyone home.

A fellowship of need,
yet each stands apart,
aloof and indifferent
to my hapless gaze
which sees
nothing

beyond the surface
of furrowed bark
I reach out to touch,
imagining I can
feel the presence
of another,

blithely oblivious
to threads of
being below,

communicating in
reciprocal circuits
of communal harmony
my selfish species
can only dream of,

whispering their ancient
secrets and signals of survival
from tree to tree
in a fellowship that
hangs by a thread.

Feeling the Heat

Glacier National Park

On the far shore of Lake McDonald
black stubble rises from the ridges
in stark reproof of fairytale forests
where trees never burn and die
lodgepole pinecones never open
bugs never burrow in wood to
feed the birds and grizzlies
scorched trunks and limbs
never break and turn to dust . . .
as smoke from a dozen new wildfires
darkens the sky
while the fever grows
the air now filled
with the toxic smell
of a grim new world
where forests may never come back
and the Magic Kingdom
burns to the bedrock

Ode to a Fake Plant

Your perfect leaves
shine back at me
as if freshly washed
by a spring rain
and make me
want to believe
in you
to touch your skin
and feel the pulse
of your artful
unblemished life
on display
in a tidy white pot
you will never outgrow
I do believe
you would thrive
in my sunless bathroom—
a perpetual plant
who never needs
watering or fussing
and would not care
if I live or die

Surprises

The soft fresh tips
of an ocotillo
have not yet learned
how to be fierce
like the barbed hooks
of a cholla that
cling to your flesh
with singular desire.

The black coachwhip snake
slashes across the trail
like an underground
crack opening
beneath your feet.

The delphinium blossoms
against the granite
stab your eyes
with hyper blue
needles.

The agave spine
pierces your skin
and burns as if
dipped in acid.

The mottled patches
of light and shadow
beneath the mesquite
suddenly become
a watching rattlesnake
tasting the wind
as you walk past it,
savoring all that
can hurt you in this
fierce bright land
where there's
nothing to fear
but the failure
to see the pain
of all things.

Teddy Bear Kingdom

Tucson Mountain Park, 2020

Hiking in solitary through desert mountains,
I enter a stand of human-sized teddy bear cactus,
clustering around me with deceptively plush stems
their arms outstretched, cloaked with dense silvery spines.
I find solace here, wishing I could touch them
to draw upon their vital strength
and know that life endures.

But their barbed claws detach readily,
and cling to flesh with fierce persistence.
They attach to any passing animal,
moving and growing wherever
conditions favor their survival,
much as this new virus spikes human cells,
hitching a ride on droplets,
flaring through our shared spaces,
tearing apart the bonds of humanity.

I tread gingerly through this new social desert,
ever mindful of invisible claws.
Desert plants we have become,
spaced wide apart,
bare soil in between.

On the Shoulders of a Giant

Saguaro National Park

Your black rotting ribs
lean upon the shoulders
of a nearby giant,
as if still carried
a while longer here
before your final
descent to earth.

Willed to Science

As I wander through this saguaro forest
of centenarians and nurse tree juveniles,
my gaze turns to the departed citizens
in different stages of death who,
unless removed by some graverobber
to become a lamp or a souvenir,
never truly leave, bodies riddled
with bullet holes or oozing black rot,
shrouded in brittle gray skin
over white spongy innards,
crumbling away to reveal
solemn silvery ribbed columns,
some sprung apart as if
there's nothing left
to hold them together,
suddenly released from
the tension of living.

Would that my body were not
promised to some medical student
I will never meet (alas)
to probe and dissect the plaques
and tangles of my brain
or whatever gets me in the end,

and that I could rest here instead
among these departed friends,
my withered innards slowly
disintegrating to reveal
my silvery ribcage
waiting for the desert
to take me back.

And wouldn't I make
a fine lamp?

Arms at Ninety-Five

What if we grew like the saguaro
and waited until fifty to grow an arm,
or not even grow one,
a lonely spear standing tall
against the sky?
Or we could wait until ninety-five,
sprouting little baby stumps
still learning to reach out
and take hold of something
worth holding.

Cause of Death Unknown

Eyes closed with white-edged wings
folded neatly across your chest
wearing your usual grayish brown suit
remarkably fresh and unruffled
considering the circumstances
you look so peaceful here
as if laid out in state
in the alleyway next to the hotel
with no mourners but me to mark
your passing from this vale of fears
so I pause for a moment to gaze
upon your still body
its spark extinguished with
no sign of struggle or blunt trauma
or anything to indicate your death
was not strictly personal
and I feel I must say a few words
about how you faced it alone
though I can only speculate
on what that was like
or your life before
and all the strife and pain
a dove must endure
like the loss of your first clutch
after the windstorm
toppled your nest
or the time that horrible boy
shot at you with his BB gun
or the Cooper's hawk

who made your life miserable
and almost got you once
but didn’t
for which I am grateful
so you could leave behind
more of your grace and beauty
than a crumpled suit of bloody feathers

Time for Sale

A juvenile Allosaur
skeleton arched
as if to freeze its
soul in lethal leap,
a mammoth's bones
slathered with
lacquer to gloss
over empty halls,
a 52-million-year-old
bird with
every feather intact
looking as if
at any moment
it might fly again,
or further back still
a mega stone panel
from Paleozoic seas
filled with trilobites
writhing in such
profusion it's hard
to believe they
wouldn't live forever—
it's all for sale at
the Fossil Show—
just run your card
and buy a piece
of time to press
like a fetish
against your soft
flesh as you dream
of eternity.

Extinction Sale

Stylishly silly two-clawed Tyrannosaurus arms
Irish elk antlers in matching intertwined sets
Great auk down so light and fluffy it disappears
Rhino horns freshly ground to cure everything
Oversized brains barely used since replaced with AI

Flowering Means Nothing

the horticulturist replied as
I pointed to the flowers
atop a crested
saguaro cactus
I had tried to save,
its life now oozing away
from necrosis within.

But tell that to a bee
who greets each flower
she meets as if
it were the first
or Mexican bats
who migrate
a thousand miles
to lap the sweet nectar
from agave
and saguaro blossoms
or the young woman
whose first flowing blood
marks the opening
of her new life
or the young country
where democracy
once bloomed.

Pluck'd in a Far-off Land

Like pilgrim's wither'd wreath of flowers
pluck'd in a far-off land.
—Lewis Carroll, *Alice in Wonderland*

They're all that remain of the journey, a descent into a dark world where no flower could possibly grow, yet there they were, glowing vivaciously in her head lamp, defying all logic and science.

She had travelled far and long to seek the dead on a silent planet whose sun had not shone for centuries, where the once thriving civilization sought shelter underground as the light of hope faded. Deep below the sand blasted stumps of once tall skyscrapers and monoliths she followed a steep lava tube, which after many miles abruptly gave way to chiseled steps and polished walls upon which symbols resembling hieroglyphs appeared, with pictures of what was obviously a sun and various objects she could not identify. But one seemed to be some kind of flower, though unlike any she had ever seen. Soon it was followed by another and another until they became the only symbol, endlessly repeated like floral exclamations. But no other trace could she find to tell the story of those who fled here below.

Exploring further, even the flower symbols died out. There was nothing more to see. She was about to turn back, but then a flash of bright colors greeted her gaze. The walls opened into a vast field of flowers of every hue and shape, growing defiantly in the pitch-black emptiness. She wandered through a dark cavern, filled with Kodachrome beds of color that blazed beneath her head lamp as far as she could see. Though their shape and structure were completely alien, she had decided to call them flowers in lieu of a better hypothesis. It was like some huge garden cathedral. There was a definite design here, with discrete paths winding among the beds. She wondered how such a thing could be possible. How could they continue to grow here without a source of light? It was as if all the last rays of the dying sun had been collected and concentrated here in these flowers to shine in the darkness for who knows how many centuries until someone would come to read a dead world's final message of what it held most dear. For a long while, she stood there, with head lamp turned off, in silent reverie. She thought of an old Greek myth about the goddess of spring, a pilgrim just like her who descended into an underworld. Suddenly she knew what she must do. She flicked on her lamp and began to pick flower after flower as she genuflected before each bed. And she made of them a wreath to honor this journey and the flowers and memories that abide.

When the Rain Comes

The spadefoot always knows
the day it will break.

No time to stay below,
the desert awakes.

Feel the thunder's hammer throw,
your long thirst to slake.

Hear the clattering crescendo—
no short-lived, sprinkly fake.

Arise with the riotous outflow,
the world is a lake.

Bask in the sunset's afterglow
and sing for the lives at stake.

Tossing Toads

I halt my mower and gently toss my neighbor
to safety from the whirling lethal blades, then
resume the ritual and repeat, saving as many as
I can, only to send them back onto a wider stage—
to be swallowed head-first by a garter snake
or stabbed by a heron, flattened by a car.
A thousand toads die as I ponder their fate.

At least the mower is quick
with not a shred of moral pretense.
No toad would die from my hand were
I not to run this infernal gas-belching
machine across this green desert.
I am but one more accomplice
to murder on a larger scale.
This blood I cannot wash from my hands.

For now, we play out our parts—
toad savior coming to the rescue of
the toad in her breeding pool
with ten thousand eggs

while deaths pile up on the stage
until at last the play is done and all
the breeding pools of life are gone
and no one's left to save any of us.

Pterodactylus

Replicated in resin
above my reading chair
your limbs and clawed
wings seem poised to
vault from the cliff and
soar over Jurassic seas.

Crestless head and tiny
body reveal you were
new to the game
but with wings unfurled
no boundary could
stop you as you
followed your prey
into a denser world.

I see the flickering
spark from your eyeless
sockets as your still weak
muscles struggled to
take off again to
keep your head
above the waves.

At last you sank into
soft sediments below where
bones became stone and
reality met immortality.[1]

---

[1] *A recent hypothesis to explain the prevalence of juvenile pterosaurs in the fossil record suggests that they might have died from drowning.*

Control

When I was five
I watched
my fish swim
round and round
in the fish bowl
as if that
were how fish
were meant
to swim.

I wanted my
animals close,
like the toy animals
I collected
in my cardboard
cage zoo.

But only real
animals would do,
so I captured
every creature
I could find
and turned it
into a specimen
to stare at
behind the glass
as I pretended
to study the real
live ways of animals.

Now they are gone
and it is me in the fishbowl,
its glass sides like my vision
closing inward as control becomes
less certain and I wish for
what every animal desires
from its very first breath.

Dethroned

It has no effect on them, the zookeeper replied,
when asked about the rhino's missing horn.
Better dehorned than dead.
Saw it off now before they come in the night
to murder and dethrone your crowning glory
to be ground into magical cure-all powder
or carved into obscene jeweled daggers
to adorn a prince's empty existence.
Just remove the profit motive.
How easy it sounds, when we pretend
to know all possible effects,
what pain is to another.
Who knows the wild heart of a rhino?
Does he still see a rhino in the pool's reflection?
Can you save the animal
without losing the soul?

Lives of a Leaf

Alchemy in green
Launch pad for a jumping spider
Wipe tissue in an emergency
Red litmus test for fall
Bare limb's dream
Leaf to litter
Black gold

Approaching Lye Brook

A few miles in from the highway
and looking much closer on the map
is a tiny wilderness known as Lye Brook.

Its name conjures up memories of a time
when farmers cut down these woods
and turned them into ashes,

leaching them and boiling their lye
in big iron pots to make potash and
reap a quick profit from the land.

As a nor'easter brought the sea to Vermont,
I stepped through a door in the morning clouds
into the soft green hills of youth.

Upslope the trail led me through
a familiar forest of ash, maple,
beech and red spruce.

The boundary of the wilderness
lay just over the next ridge
or maybe the next after that.

It did not matter.
When you hike toward wilderness
new visions start to unfold.

Eliot Porter portraits of leaves
bleed their colors beneath me
and shoot up into my veins.

With bony fingers, a sapling
clings to the crimson leaves
as if it must not lose them.

These are Robert Frost woods,
lovely, dark and deep—perhaps
deeper than I care to go.

The trail crosses a small ravine with
plunging brook that taunts me
to jump across its turbulence.

Uncertainly I leap.
I am not the same jumper of late,
but I make it, this time.

With adrenaline coursing,
I stride through the woods,
reliving all my connections.

These woods I carry with me—
I could hike here with eyes closed.
I come not for new vistas but to touch again:

the scaly skin of lichens on beech;
the softness of moss on boulders;
the furrowed faces in bark . . .

I rekindle these images,
clutching them tightly as
tree roots to granite.

And in the sheltering darkness
I see my mother's final journey
as not too different from my own.

Grasping at the fading canvases,
she stowed them away in crevasses
unknown, to feed her heart again.

What adventures she must have relived
until the figments fragmented
and her neurons flashed no more.

I see her walking the dawn streets of childhood,
feeling the touch of flesh and earth until
that last leap into the failing waters.

The clouds thicken and I must return.
The woods grow dimmer
and smell of ashes.

The wildness of Lye Brook
lies just over the next ridge—
but it can wait.

Holy Ghost on a Window

A thump from outside invaded
my melancholy this morning.
I looked up in time to see
the banded tail of a Cooper's hawk
clutching its limp prize while
taking wing from the patio.

Then I noticed a pale outline
in one of the large windows.
Drawn in whitish film were
wings, head and one clawed foot
clearly visible in stark detail.

I marveled at the fine traceries of
imbrued feathers pressed into glass,
like the silhouettes of lost souls
imprinted on eternity by nuclear blast.
There was even the bill and eye socket
looking inward with vacuous stare.

The upturned wings called to mind
stained glass images of God
the Third Person of the Trinity,
with tiny rays streaking out
from where the impact splattered
its body against the fatal mirror.

I knew it was a mourning dove
and not God that was dead.

But framed by a green juniper,
the shroud in the glass
made a fitting portrait
of all the cemeteries I've known,
with their empty promises
that scatter like feathers
blowing from the patio—
leaving no trace save
a thump that still echoes.

A Terrible Beauty

Swatting flies from my pizza
reminds me of a wildflower
some call stinkin' Benjamin
whose dark red flowers
look and smell like
rotting slabs of fetid flesh,
capitalizing on carrion flies
to carry out its secret mission to
pollinate and perpetuate
the species . . .
while this less adaptable creature
swats in futility and
contemplates nature's
formidable beauty.

Evolution

You start out simply
with two short sounds
but the way you shout
that third syllable
leaves no doubt you're
the kind who likes
to shake things up
and start something new

Ode to Lucy

On viewing Lucy, an Australopithecus afarensis fossil on display at Lucy's Legacy Exhibition, Houston Museum of Natural Science, 2007

Who will I discover in my family tree?
Perhaps there's royalty in my blood,
some famous inventor or celebrity,
some brave soldier who died in the mud.

On a trip to Houston, I found my answer.
In a dim lit room, there you were—
your face budding like a dawn flower
from a branch of our chromosome tower.

Arrayed in glass-fronted coffin, your bones
burned into my vision like precious stones—
fragments of forearm, ribs, skull, and jaw
in the scant remains of you that I saw.

On one side is a model
of you staring back at me.
Like us, you were bipedal,
walking upright, hands free.

Three-and-a-half feet tall you once stood,
with a pelvis that proved you were female.
If I could meet you in your ancient wood,
would you perceive me as a primate male?

Would there be some glimmer of recognition
from your apelike visage—a look of wonder
as if you've seen an apparition,
something from the world yonder?

Lucy, your grave robbers called you—
Lucy in the Sky—a fitting name
for someone who knew
how to play the survival game.

Though your brain was smaller than mine,
it was big enough for you and your clan
to last a hundred thousand years times nine—
far better than my human brand.

You had to grow up fast,
with little time for play.
Your challenges were vast
through the long night and day.

Unlike us, you were a swinger,
with strong arms and curved fingers,
who moved with grace and ease
on land and through the trees.

I would find it hard to live in a tree.
But perhaps living in two spaces
was your secret. Up there you could flee
your enemies as you sought out new places.

Forever I will see your face,
your strong jutting jaw and flat nose,
speaking to me from that honored place
in our family gallery with elegant pose.

Through your genetic wisdom
you taught us to climb high
while preparing our kingdom
on the ground nearby.

I see no blue blood or royalty
in that face, just your beautiful humanity
beaming back at me from beyond
across the eons.

There should be a constellation for you—
twinkling diamonds in the sky—
so that we may look up from our branch anew
and celebrate our family tie.

By Different Boats

I care not a whit for my ancestry
or the look of my great
grandfather as a boy.
I find no comfort in faces
or names like mine.

I do not cling to the cluster of genes
carried across the waters in blue-eyed
vessels without my vote.

But give me a gorilla,
now there's a face I can relate to,
the way he looks at me
from behind the glass
and makes me see
there's a link I can feel
down to my bones,
though we got here by
different boats.

Distress

Golden brown, the female sea lion
stretched out in front of me
along the shoreline, her body
set off by four traffic cones
and two women warning me
not to walk too close
lest I add to her distress.

She had been there since dawn,
and did not seem injured.
Occasionally she would raise a flipper
or turn her head to gaze at the ocean,
but something held her back.
Was she ready to give birth?
Or had the waters suddenly become too deep?
Did a memory still burn too fiercely,
perhaps a narrow miss by a propeller
or a great white shark?

I stared from a respectful distance,
close enough to see into her eyes,
pretending they looked back at me
with all the sadness of the sea,
though I knew full well they
look at everyone that way,
her mind's dark secrets
a mystery.

Far removed from the La Jolla Cove
spectacle of barking sea lions
and yapping tourists, it was just
an inscrutable moment
between me and one sea lion
sharing the common anxiety
of where the next blow will fall,
trying to make sense of it all.

Thermoregulation

Sluggishly, the lizard basks in the early sun,
deftly shifting in and out of the shade
to keep her body temperature
on an even keel, as her blood
slowly quickens.

Masters of self-regulation, we sapien
primates still overheat and freeze.
Confident of our thermostats,
we seek and defy the sun,
ignoring the signs
that our bodies are baking,
or retreat to our rooms
and slip into cold sleep forever
in a land of opportunity for
everyone but those who
cannot pay their heating bills.

Minds too can overheat and freeze.
when the temperature of emotion
moves us too fast or too slow
and we do things
against our best interests.

We avoid when we should approach,
attack when we should embrace.

If only we could deftly shift
like the lizard in and out of
the shades of our emotions.

What Kind of Man

A heavyset man, leaning on his cane,
he sidled up to me at the bus stop,
with a story to tell.

He pointed to the gutter.
Can you believe it?
Right here across from the hospital—
a Gila monster! A big fella.
He spread his arms wide.

There was only one thing to do,
so he grabbed it behind the head and carried it
safely to the surrounding desert hills.
Of course, I was late for my appointment,
he said, then let out a belly laugh.

I smiled and thanked him
as I boarded the bus.
And all the way home I wondered
what kind of man
walks this earth
with a connection so strong
to all that lives
that he would rescue
a monster from the gutter
and save this wretched soul
from despair.

Canyon Stories

James House, Ramsey Canyon, Arizona

The way it sets into
the south-facing slope
above the floodplain
and its faded boards
softly weather in the sun,
how it blends
into the forest
like a fallen tree—
a gentle reminder
of settlers' brief reign.
But in the setting sun
long shadows of
their rough ways
still linger . . .

blasting a toll road
through the canyon
to build their mining
camp with dance hall
and saloons;
channeling the creek
into twisted contortions
and narrow channels
to water their orchards
while choking out
riparian trees;
hunting the wildlife

and ignoring the richness
of its diversity;
slashing oak, pine, and fir
from the mountaintops
to graze their livestock
while suppressing
cool fires that swept
the forest floor of
small trees and debris;
scouring the slopes of their
minerals while seeding
what's left with false claims
and when it is all spent
leaving the hillside
to its barren solitude.

Sycamores, oaks, and
junipers now press
against the rotting walls
where spiny lizards
bask in the dappled sun.
The wind blows clean
through the forest
and the creek
flows free again.

Sanctuary

Whitewater Draw, McNeal, Arizona

I come for the spectacle—
twenty thousand sandhill cranes
honking their hosannas
in exuberant profusion.

I view from afar
as they alight and crowd into position
standing shoulder to shoulder
in the shallow waters,
temporarily safe from
all that might harm them—
a migrant city of birds
flying forth each morning
to eke out their living in
surrounding fields of corn,
then returning to wait out
the dark in the safety
of their wet roost.

A small group emerges
from the nearby marsh grass,
much closer this time, as if
finally accepting my presence,
loafing at their ease, in casual
strides, sometimes jumping
and facing off in animated conversations
and flashes of red forehead.

They watch me as well,
fellow migrant species from the Pleistocene,
whose ancestors followed
the ebb and flow of ice sheets
as the oceans rose and fell.

Will the great birds still soar on high
through future skies in solemn witness
to the spectacle of my descendants
huddling shoulder to shoulder
in the rising waters
of a hungry sea?

Shades from the Chasm

Gazing down at Bright Angel Trail,
I see no angels here—
only shades from the chasm:
hikers dutifully descending into hells of their own creation,
then plodding upward again, as in a Doré Purgatory,
naked terraces laid down long ago
like the backbones of ancient sea creatures,
swallows darting across the layers
like thoughts too fleet to recall,
splashes of red in the receding scarps of canyon walls—
wounds of a bleeding Earth.

Perceptible Increments

I watch the shadow cast from my apartment
descend with the rising sun in barely perceptible increments
notable to no one but me and wonder how many more
notable things have I missed simply because they move
too slowly or that I lack the right perspective.

What if I could observe the Earth suspended in space
and watch it move in grace like a blue goddess
against a sea of stars?

What if I could see the Earth wake up and breathe
as spring comes to the Northern Hemisphere
with a growing carpet of green?

What if I could be there through every epoch and era
to witness the slow progression of life unfold
in rapid motion on a hundred screens at once,
only to see them one by one go blank
in the Sixth Great Mass Extinction?

What if I could watch the Sahara sands creep southward
consuming the rainforests and farms of Africa
as a hungry tide of humanity spreads northward?

What if I could watch the oceans rise and swallow
one island nation after another until they
lap on the shores of Kensington and Times Square?

What if I could watch the mountain glaciers retreat,
in barely perceptible increments, as they solemnly
ascend the slopes into thin air?

Plea for an Imaginary Amphibian

but nothing is real
until it can be sold
—W.S. Merwin, Journey

What is the price of the Milky Way?
Think of a number.
Any day now black holes
will be sold like donuts
and dark matter
the ultimate investment opportunity.

Just imagine an alternate universe
that could be yours.
Everything is on the table,
even the things we thought were
non-negotiable.

But can we not keep some creatures
from this marketplace?
Let us keep at least our
imaginary friends and toads.

To See Further

I look upon the first deep field image
of the James Webb Space Telescope,
where galaxies dance with dark matter,
bending and magnifying the light
from behind them
revealing more distant galaxies
barely out of the Big Bang cradle,
no more than diffuse clouds
of bright glowing buds
still learning to feel their way
through time's arrow
before spiraling out
into the future.

But will our newfound eyes
ever allow us to see with
the perspective of a galaxy—
an entity as old as time itself—
when we still cannot see
as a tree or a mollusk sees,
or see beyond the dark matter
still obscuring the universe
inside each of us?

We need new eyes
to see what we are seeing—
eyes not of gold-plated beryllium
but of some rarer stuff,
not high in space
but from a deeper place,

to penetrate the atmosphere
of our sensory bubbles
and see the world
in a new light
beyond the spectrum.

One More Vision

Only once have I seen one,
its slender outline
slowly crystallizing against
a perfect camouflage
of green undergrowth.
In a flash of perception
a smooth green snake appeared.
I reached out to grab it
as if to seize an apparition.
The little snake squirmed
but did not bite me
with its tiny insectivorous
jaws and teeth.

Sixty years have passed,
yet its emerald green
still burns with
delightful intensity
unlike the book I just read
that I can barely recall.
What peculiar enchantment
still holds me in the spell
of that rare moment?

I look to the earth
hoping for
one more vision.

Future Portrait of Dark Matter

Someday, an artist will paint it
and it will hang in plain view
in a distant gallery.
Don't worry if, at first,
all you see is a gilt frame
surrounding black space.
Look deeper and you begin
to feel a presence there,
pulling you inward.
You notice faint rings
and arcs of light appear
and a slight twitching
in the fabric
as if to signal there's
more to the picture
hidden behind the canvas.
Draw closer now
and you will see
its true face
as everything
stretches apart
and goes dark.

Untainted

After the character Anne Clayborne, a geologist opposed to terraforming, from Red Mars *by Kim Stanley Robinson*

If life proves to be the rule
rather than the exception,
most precious are the places
where nothing ever dies
and matter never tries
to breathe or reproduce
and become something it's not—
an ageless dance of
inorganic animation,
uplifting, flowing, and eroding
in fractured monumental sculptures,
crystalline flowers
and mineral-stained murals—
a pristine place where
no one has gone before
and never will,
untainted by life's
original sin.

Reenactment

The battle is won or lost,
never over, perpetually replayed
with resurrected dead heroes,
as we revel in the tempests
of our travails.

But the battle for the planet
we once knew is over,
as we burn the future
and fiddle our feckless tunes.

There will be no reenactment,
for what field or country
is big enough to stage it?
What hymns or words
strong enough to emote
the horror of our inaction?

There will be no
resurrection, no
revel in the tempest.

CENTOS

Cento: From the Latin for "patchwork garment," a poetic form composed entirely of lines from poems by other poets

I Am the Earth

Mother of all the manifold forms of life,
we can hardly grasp it:
barnacles . . . cling to sunken ledges,
worms crawl to wander about the black earth's intestines,
the hummingbird shimmers . . . the katydid works her
chromatic reed.
All the strange parts fit together.
Nothing in the world is single.
We are not souls but systems, and we move in clouds of our
    unknowing.
I am the Earth and the Earth is me.[2]

---

[2] *With lines (in order of appearance) by Henry Van Dyke, Margaret Atwood, Wilbert Snow, Aratus, Walt Whitman, Alberto Rios, Percy Bysshe Shelley, Stanley Kunitz, and Jane Yolen*

Nature's First Poem

I speak of underneathedness and the welcome of mosses,
the silk upon the mushroom's underside,
this spare, hidden beauty all around
from the red mold and slimy roots of earth
where Nature's wildest genius reigns.
O sweet spontaneous earth.
This is the first poem.
The Poetry of earth is never *dead.*[3]

---

[3] *With lines (in order of appearance) by Camille T. Dungy, Elinor Wylie, Lizette Woodworth Reese, William Cullen Bryant, Philip Freneau, e.e. cummings, Mark Van Doren, and John Keats*

A Special Fabric

The animals have come down from the hills—
a black shambling bear,
the bat that flits at close of eve,
black-footed ferrets disappear into holes,
the faintest freckles on the hide of fawns.
In the slight ripple, the fishes dart like fingers.
Frogs chug throaty songs.
Flounders flit beneath your feet.
A narrow Fellow in the Grass, a Whip Lash unbraiding in the
 Sun,
a modest animal . . . neither beautiful nor ugly but merely
 alive—
something different, which is always difficult to embrace.
These creatures that I briefly move among—
a special fabric, they are all one flesh.
Let the snake wait under his weed.[4]

---

[4] *With lines (in order of appearance) by Stephen Dunn, Lucille Clifton, William Blake, Harry Crosby, Elinor Wylie, Delmore Schwartz, Allison Adelle Hedge Coke, Wilbert Snow, Emily Dickinson, Tony Hoagland, Alberto Rios, Marilyn L. Taylor, Gertrude Stein, and William Carlos Williams*

If I Break into Blossom

It doesn't have to be the blue iris, it could be weeds in a vacant lot,
marvels undreamed of suddenly unfold—
sunflowers turning toward the light,
wild plum-trees in tremulous white,
the frail duration of a flower.
If I bow, it is in recognition of true being.
I would break into blossom.[5]

[5] *With lines (in order of appearance) by Mary Oliver, Wilbert Snow, Dylan Thomas, Sara Teasdale, Philip Freneau, Alfred Kreymborg, and James Wright*

The Violet's Breath

A slime of green algae . . . so we are here in this plant-created
oxygen,
the earth breathing.
I inhaled the violet's breath.[6]

---

[6] *With lines (in order of appearance) by A.R. Ammons, Richard Eberhart, and Ralph Waldo Emerson*

The Way to the Sea

I sift the sand through my fingers,
and in the swaddlings of the waves,
I hear . . . the windy beating of the sea.
Listen! you hear the grating roar of pebbles which the waves
draw back, and fling.
The breakers . . . spout like white whales on an Arctic sea.
There is a wide, wide wonder in it all,
water astonishing and difficult altogether.
All the sounds of the living beings and inanimate things,
the world with all her winds and waters, earth and air,
an earlier world in sure command giving the orders.
The Ocean has its silent caves, deep, quiet, and alone.
The river knows the way to the sea.[7]

---

[7] *With lines (in order of appearance) by Charles Erskine Scott Wood, May Swenson, Amy Lowell, Matthew Arnold, Wilbert Snow, James Weldon Johnson, Gertrude Stein, Arturo Giovannitti, John Hall Wheelock, Claude McKay, Nathaniel Hawthorne, and Ralph Waldo Emerson*

Thirst Is All I Know

Lonely, open, vast and free, the dark'ning desert lies.
Deep arroyos boldly trace the paths where sudden waters run.
The desert sees itself through . . . antelope eyes, hummingbird, fox, lizard, vulture.
They cannot scare me with their empty spaces.
I'd rather be here than any place I know—
oh that the desert were my dwelling place.
You taught me how to live without the rain. You are thirst and thirst is all I know.
I am the desert. I am free.
And there I found myself more truly and more strange.[8]

---

[8] *With lines (in order of appearance) by Bertrand N. O. Walker, Diane Siebert, David Hinton, Robert Frost, W.C. Handy, Lord Byron, Benjamin Alire Sáenz, Diane Siebert, and Wallace Stevens*

When You Are Fallen

An elegant use of foliage and grace,
you are the skin of our terrain . . . our democracy.
The wind moves slowly in the branches.
What will I do when you are fallen?
The stunted trees look sick.
Where lies the leaf-caught world once thought abiding?
I can hear underground, that sucking and sobbing,
like a tree wondering what happened to the forest.
Darkness spills across the sky like an oil plume,
as the trees are rushing to warn us again.[9]

---

[9] *With lines (in order of appearance) by Gertrude Stein, Sharon Olds, Wallace Stevens, May Swenson, Ralph Waldo Emerson, Louise Bogan, Theodore Roethke, Tony Hoagland, Craig Santos Perez, and Charles Simic*

When Beauty Lived and Died

A . . . face with nature's own hand painted,
the rarities of nature's truth.
So great a sum of sums,
. . . as food to life,
or as sweet-seasoned showers are to the ground.
So oft have I invoked thee for my muse.
So long as eyes can see, so long lives this—
when yellow leaves, or none, or few, do hang
upon those boughs which shake against the cold,
when beauty lived and died as flowers do now.
A map doth nature store,
to show false art what beauty was of yore.
Our minutes hasten to their end
as the waves make towards the pebbl'd shore.[10]

---

[10] *With lines from Shakespeare's sonnets*

Little Deaths

We devastate them unreligiously.
How easy it is to live with little deaths.
I cannot help but wonder at
the water strider setting out across the water, long-legged and
    light as a breath,
two termites' curious self-perpetuating bodies . . .
to live again a butterfly.
Where do you suppose they've gone the bees now?
Wouldn't you think the bees had suffered enough?
The silent rounds of . . . roaches begin.[11]

---

[11] *With lines (in order of appearance) by Ralph Waldo Emerson, Robert Wrigley, Ogden Nash, Ted Kooser, Stephanie Burt, Christina Rossetti, David Baker, Mona Van Duyn, and Charles Reznikoff*

Oh Children

Too bad you weren't here six months ago . . . you could have
seen
the blue booby . . . gather the blue objects of the world,
orange orioles hop like music-box birds and sing,
the bird's fire-fangled feathers dangle down,
brightly plumed jays . . . fly as if hung in one place like
pinwheels,
the owl that calls upon the night,
and swallows circling with their shimmering sound—
these beautiful wild untamable creatures,
a song out of imagining.
Oh children, will you grow up in a world without birds?[12]

---

[12] *With lines (in order of appearance) by Billy Collins, James Tate, Amy Lowell, Wallace Stevens, Allison Adelle Hedge Coke, William Blake, Sara Teasdale, Marsden Hartley, Louis Zukofsky, and Margaret Atwood*

Never Again the Same

The mockingbird sounds his delicious gurgles, cackles,
    screams, weeps.
The wild warblers are warbling in the jungle.
And then, frail, exquisite, afar, a hermit-thrush.
I do not think that they will sing to me—
the woodcock's watery call . . . the note the white-throat utters.
Never again would birds' song be the same.
Where are the songs of Spring?[13]

---

[13] *With lines (in order of appearance) by Walt Whitman, Wallace Stevens, Angelina Weld Grimké, T.S. Eliot, Edna St. Vincent Millay, Robert Frost, and John Keats*

A Minor House

The earth says have a place, be what that place requires.
You build yourselves immense houses to live in, and you are afraid even there.
The house-wreckers have left the door and a staircase, now leading to the empty room of night.
Repairs? But how can one begin?
The great structure has become a minor house,
something gray and dull and limited,
this damaged longing like a heavy piece of furniture inside you,
seeking . . . some resting flower of yesterday's delight.[14]

---

[14] *With lines (in order of appearance) by William Stafford, Emanuel Carnevali, Charles Reznikoff, Weldon Kees, Wallace Stevens, Alberto Rios, Tony Hoagland, and Robert Frost*

We Once Had Tuskers

Imponderable the dinosaur sinks slow.
I see the bones of those who have existed as I now exist,
a world lost.
Never shall the chemistry of the secret earth restore.

Polar bears they'll read about like dinosaurs.
How many millipedes or elephants are left?
The tender creatures who have been taken from us all
. . . like drops of water on a stove—a hiss and gone.
They are all gone away.
I will not look at them again.

Everything once had a soul, even this clam . . . you needed to
take care.
There is a circle will not close.
So Eden sank to grief.
Sing the saddest kind of song
. . . how the elephants have died. *We once had tuskers.*
We die with the dying: see, they depart, and we go with them.
Rage, rage against the dying of the light.[15]

---

[15] *With lines (in order of appearance) by Hart Crane, Charles Erskine Scott Wood, William Carlos Williams, Edna St. Vincent Millay, Laura Cresté, Archibald Lampman, Alberto Rios, Charles Reznikoff, Edwin Arlington Robinson, Gertrude Stein, Margaret Atwood, Rhina P. Espaillat, Robert Frost, Johnny Mercer, Stephen Derwent Partington, T.S. Eliot, and Dylan Thomas*

A Diminished Thing

A song out of imagining,
mystery made visible.
Once the world was perfect, and we were happy in that world.
What shall I remember?
The plants, the rivers, the mountains and the endless plain;
the immense elephant of things;
the sea cows the Great Auks the gorillas;
the frail duration of a flower;
the power of your intense fragility;
how we've all dwindled.
What to make of a diminished thing?[16]

[16] *With lines (in order of appearance) by Louis Zukofsky, Richard Eberhart, Joy Harjo, Edmund Wilson, Langston Hughes, Alberto Rios, W.S. Merwin, Philip Freneau, e.e. cummings, Margaret Atwood, and Robert Frost*

The Usual Hokum

How we've all dwindled, we are a dying symphony.
We speak through sickly smiles . . . the grim joke and the
banal resolution
with the usual human hokum.
This is the season of our lonely dreams.
We are locked out: like children seeking love.
And now the sky is empty of birds.
Pretty soon you got used to it always being that way.
Who next will drop and disappear?
Tell him that it is we who are important.
So was produced this tragedy.
This is where all our joyrides ended.[17]

---

[17] *With lines (in order of appearance) by Margaret Atwood, Karl Shapiro, Don Marquis, William Ellery Leonard, George Oppen, W. Todd Kaneko, Stephen Vincent Benet, William Wordsworth, W.S. Merwin, Allen Tate, and Charles Simic*

A Comfortable Disease

You look upon the earth,
it was enough for anyone to love for all a lifetime.
But nothing is real until it can be sold.
Progress is a comfortable disease.
I run, I run to the whistle of money.
A surfeit had I, now am bound to a ghost's wealth—
something in me is lost, forever lost,
this soul, this vanity, flown hither and thither.
What did I get in exchange for my little bargain? What did I
    lose?
And would it have been worth it, after all?
The hour of light is brief, then decays.
So dawn goes down to day.
The world is my oyster no more.[18]

---

[18] *With lines (in order of appearance) by Louise Bogan, Robert Francis, W.S. Merwin, e.e. cummings, Theodore Roethke, Lizette Woodworth Reese, Claude McKay, Elinor Wylie, Tony Hoagland, T.S. Eliot, Allen Tate, Robert Frost, and Ira Gershwin*

A Terrible Stain

Something went wrong, they say.
Beneath its canopy of poisoned air,
the river sweats oil and tar.
There will come soft rains and the smell of the ground.
The waste remains, the waste remains and kills,
like a terrible stain soaked into the sheets, so deep that nothing
    will ever get it out.
The difference is spreading,
but wotthehell wothtehell.[19]

---

[19] *With lines (in order of appearance) by Ted Kooser, Carolyn Kizer, T.S. Eliot, Sara Teasdale, William Empson, Tony Hoagland, Gertrude Stein, and Don Marquis*

Watch Us Burn

In a dark time, the eye begins to see,
cold dark deep and absolutely clear.
How to fuel the world, then die.
It gives a lovely light!
We smile all the time now, smiles of the lobotomized, and the
    world fries,
no matter how many warnings we have heard.
The facts were told not to speak and were taken away.
Time will say nothing but I told you so.
After such knowledge, what forgiveness?
I can't forget this rage, I don't know what to do with it.
They tell me you are wicked and I believe them.
I have no language, hardly any word to name you with.
To hell with you . . . you will rot and be blown through the
    next solar system.
Watch us burn: possible epitaph.[20]

---

[20] *With lines (in order of appearance) by Theodore Roethke, Elizabeth Bishop, Anne Waldman, Edna St. Vincent Millay, Margaret Atwood, Alberto Rios, Jane Hirshfield, W.H. Auden, T.S. Eliot, Rafael Campo, Carl Sandburg, Witter Bynner, William Carlos Williams, and Angélica Freitas*

The Beautiful Enormous Dawns of Time

Five billion miles away, a galaxy dies like a snowflake falling
on water.
The earth goes round a corner,
not one will care at last when it is done.
There is nothing left of this world . . .
without birdsong, without any hopeful yellow flower.
The lichens grow by spreading, gray, concentric shocks,
will one by one engrave themselves on silence
and the beautiful enormous dawns of time, after we perish.[21]

---

[21] *With lines (in order of appearance) by Ted Kooser, Tony Hoagland, Sara Teasdale, e.e. cummings, Stephen Dunn, Elizabeth Bishop, Abdellatif Laâbi, and Robinson Jeffers*

About the Author

Gene Twaronite is the author of thirteen books, including six poetry collections and seven works of fiction and nonfiction. His first poetry book, *Trash Picker on Mars* (Kelsay Books), won the 2017 New Mexico-Arizona Book Award for poetry. He is a former Writer-in-Residence for Pima County Public Library.

A native New Englander, Gene now lives in Tucson, a desert city where, in the words of Wallace Stevens, he found himself "more truly and more strange." Whether writing about lizards, cacti, trees, or toads—imaginary or otherwise—his relation to the natural world has always been a central part of his writing. He has a B.S. in Natural Resources and a M.A. in Education and taught junior high science in private and public schools.

Together with his wife, Jo Kelleher, he established New Hampshire Audubon's Scotland Brook Wildlife Sanctuary in northern NH, where he sometimes woke up to see a moose munching on his garden. He's a retired Horticultural Specialist for Arizona State University and a Senior Instructional Specialist for the University of Arizona, where he taught how to create safer, fire-resilient landscapes in this warming new world of increasing wildfires.

Follow more of Gene's writing at his website:
genetwaronitepoet.com

www.ingramcontent.com/pod-product-compliance
Lightning Source LLC
LaVergne TN
LVHW020652100826
845148LV00012B/2444

* 9 7 9 8 9 0 1 4 6 9 7 2 9 *